Daring to Dream

Hazel Wood Waterman, c. 1920 (San Diego Historical Society).

Daring to Dream

The Life of

Hazel Wood Waterman

by

Sally Bullard Thornton

SAN DIEGO HISTORICAL SOCIETY

Library of Congress Cataloging in Publication Data
Thornton, Sally Bullard
  Daring to Dream: the life of Hazel Wood Waterman /
by Sally Bullard Thornton.
    118 pp.
  Bibliography: p. 107
  Includes index.
  ISBN 0-918740-06-1
  ISBN 0-918740-07-X (pbk.)
    1. Waterman, Hazel Wood, 1865-1948.   2. Architects—
California—Biography.   3. Architecture, Modern—20th
century—California—San Diego.   4. Architecture—
California—San Diego.   5. San Diego (Calif.)—Buildings,
structures, etc.   I. Title.
NA737.W38T48 1987
720′.92′4—dc19
[B]   87-26507
                                                                      CIP

Designed by Thomas L. Scharf

Printed in the United States of America
by Arts and Crafts Press
San Diego, California

For
John, Mark and Steven

Contents

Illustrations

Foreword

During the relatively short history of architecture in California, a few persons already stand out as notable — individuals whose work has withstood the test of time and may now be called classic. To those familiar with this history, the names of Bernard Maybeck, Irving Gill, William Hebbard, William Templeton Johnson, the Greene brothers, Richard Neutra and Cliff May are legendary. What these architects share, however, as their most common trait — other than outstanding work — is their sex: male. Where, one might ask are the female members of this profession?

The contribution of women to the field of California architecture began late but has made lengthy strides because of the ground-breaking efforts of a few brilliant pioneers. Certainly Julia Morgan stands out for giving us the incredible legacy of San Simeon built for William Randolph Hearst. Travellers to northern San Diego County can see the work of another pioneer, Lillian Rice, whose romantic idealism took shape in the beautiful Spanish-style homes of Rancho Santa Fe.

Hazel Wood Waterman ranks with the best of these early leaders. An all-encompassing designer, she not only melded the basic architectural elements of her buildings, but worked for a complete style, one that included interior colors, furnishings, window treatments, and garden plans. Hers was a philosophy of total site development to provide the greatest comfort for her clients. Her dreams became a reality in San Diego. But what is remarkable about Hazel Wood Waterman is that she began her career in the latter half of her life. She was a widow, a single parent rearing three children. Yet she dared to do something not usual for her sex, and did it well — much to the admiration of her peers, both men and women.

What is remarkable about Sally Bullard Thornton is that she, too, began her career as a writer later in life. Well known for her leadership in the cultural community, she, like Hazel Waterman, has dared to dream and to provide in this book an insightful look at San Diego's first woman architect. She has taken her subject through a fascinating life in Berkeley, Julian, and finally San Diego, where Hazel, among her many accomplishments, designed Sally's own childhood home on Curlew Street. In this book, author and subject have merged in a delightful and productive way.

Iris H.W. Engstrand, Ph.D.
University of San Diego

Preface

In the field of architecture, women have been less encouraged to participate on a competitive basis with their male counterparts. Hazel Wood Waterman, however, stands apart as an exceptional woman who was encouraged to pursue such a career by Irving Gill, a leading young San Diego architect in the first half of the twentieth century. Her success story has special significance since she represents the relatively untrained — only one year of university study — middle-aged mother who suddenly becomes a single parent and head of the household.

Because there were no architectural schools in the area, Hazel Waterman enhanced her skills by taking correspondence courses and accepting assignments from a local architectural firm while raising her young family. As she became more proficient, Hazel was commissioned by friends and acquaintances who were impressed by her apparent knowledge and sympathetic understanding of their needs. She delighted clients by her perception and willingness to adapt to their requirements. Hazel often extended the breadth of their thinking to enhance the final product. She felt that an attractive and appropriate interior was essential to the total concept of well designed and arranged rooms. Hazel also placed importance on the development of the structure's exterior design which included the garden landscape and selection of plants.

Hazel Waterman did not limit herself to domestic or residential architecture. One of her most significant, acclaimed contributions was the restoration of the Casa de Estudillo, one of the oldest buildings in Old Town, San Diego. After exhaustive research, she created one of the most historically correct adobe reproductions in the area. Hazel's perfectionism was revealed by the observor's inability to detect the old existing remnants from the newly constructed extension of the house. Although she did not design a large number of structures, Hazel was most noted for quality and care in the specifics or finer points of her work.

The story of this intriguing lady begins when she marries a mining engineer, son of California's seventeenth governor. Hazel goes with him to a new life in a rough, remote, little mining town located sixty miles northeast of San Diego. There her husband deals with the problems of running his father's mine and other holdings. During that time, Hazel gradually adjusted to a life in contrast to her pre-marital years as the daughter of a Protestant minister, school teacher, administrator, and publisher.

Later, her life changes again when Hazel and her young family move to San Diego. They are beset by more problems and financial hardships when the governor passes away. Living in the city allows Hazel and her husband to enrich their intellectual lives together. They also cultivate new friendships which help sustain Hazel when her husband dies suddenly.

Hazel shows us how she survives by setting goals with the highest of standards. She sets an excellent example with her fine intelligence, determination, and drive to persevere in the achievement of success. Hazel Wood Waterman dared to dream and to extend herself beyond the expected stereotypical mother-housewife role of the day. She taught herself to become self sufficient without sacrificing her gentility.

Sally Bullard Thornton
San Diego, California
August 1, 1987

Acknowledgements

My grateful thanks and deep appreciation go to Dr. Iris H.W. Engstrand, Dr. Raymond S. Brandes and Dr. James R. Moriarty, III of the University of San Diego for their insight, expertise, inspiration and diligent assistance during the research and preparation of this volume.

My thanks also go to the staff of the San Diego Historical Society, particularly Sylvia Arden, Head Librarian and Archivist, Bruce Kamerling, Curator of Collections, Larry Booth, Curator of Photographic Collections, and Jane Booth, Photo Archivist; to Rhoda Kruse of the California Room of the San Diego Public Library; to Mary Belcher Farrell, Elizabeth Hill Carson, Legler H. Benbough and others who shared their memories with me.

My gratitude as well goes to Elinor Savage Oatman, past president of the Wednesday Club; Clara Breed, Wednesday Club Librarian and former Librarian of the San Diego Public Library; and Dr. Steven Schoenherr, Professor of History, University of San Diego.

My appreciation to Bonnie Hardwick, Head of Manuscripts Division, Lawrence Dinnean, Curator of Pictorial Collections, and Marie Thornton, Staff Member, The Bancroft Library, and William R. Roberts, University Archivist, University of California, Berkeley; Bill Jones, Librarian, and Sarah Blakeslee, Special Collections Department, California State University, Chico; Irene Gibbs, deceased, former club resident, and Marianne Payovich, Manager, Berkeley City Women's Club.

Most importantly, a special thanks must go to my friend, editor, and designer, Thomas L. Scharf, who put this book together so beautifully.

Finally, I appreciate my husband John and our sons Mark and Steven, who gave me their love, patience, understanding, and encouragement.

REV. AND MRS. JESSE WOOD AND THEIR CHILDREN.

Magnolia, Jessamine, Earnest, Hazel, Tison, Honor, Walton, Eugenia, Alice May, Willie. (Mrs. B. A. Grecia)

The Wood Family (Special Collections, Meriam Library, California State University, Chico).

Chapter One
Family Heritage

On February 24, 1903, just two and one-half months before her thirty-eighth birthday, Hazel Wood Waterman lost the love of her life, husband Waldo Sprague Waterman. The shock and reality of what had happened whirled in Hazel's mind. She reviewed the events of her life and made some decisions about the future. At this point, Hazel Waterman, widow and mother of three, came to her most important conclusion — to pursue a career in architecture.[1]

Hazel had married Waldo, the bright son of the governor of California, on April 11, 1889, three years after he was graduated from the University of California at Berkeley. They first met on the Berkeley campus where she studied art and design, and he specialized in mining engineering. Previously, in May, 1887, Waldo had married Myra Pauline Benfry. The union lasted about five months; Myra became ill suddenly and passed away on October 24.[2] After an appropriate mourning period, Waldo renewed his acquaintance with Hazel. They had shared a number of activities at Berkeley, then a small campus. Waldo was business manager of the yearbook and heavily involved in university life.[3] His friendship with Hazel led to their courtship and subsequent marriage.

Hazel Wood was born on the fifth of May, 1865, in the little town of Tuskegee, Alabama. Her father, Jesse Wood, served as president of the Tuskegee Female College until the end of the Civil War. Following the war, Wood pursued his career as a Methodist minister until early 1868, when he took the family to California. They settled in the Central Valley area where Wood, working as a minister, teacher, county clerk, and superintendent of public schools, supported his wife and ten children.[4]

Jesse Wood, the son of a well-to-do farmer, was born on October 29, 1839, in Appling, Columbia County, Georgia. His mother remarried when he was ten years old. Wood's stepfather, William E. Price, who moved the family to Barbour County, Alabama, was responsible for Jesse's education at the Academy and High School of Glenville. Wood entered the junior class of Emory and Henry College, Virginia, in August, 1857. He tutored in mathematics during his senior year and was graduated June 8, 1859.[5]

Wood received a license to preach in the Methodist Church ministry on October 8, 1859, and was appointed to Union Springs, after admission to the Alabama conference in December, 1860. He married Alice Catherine Tison, a graduate of the Glenville female seminary, on January 29, 1861. Alice's parents, James G. and Adriana (Ott) Tison, were natives of South Carolina. Wood became Tuskegee College President in 1863 and subsequently the Tuskegee Circuit minister at Auburn Station.[6]

Wood arrived with his family in San Francisco, via the Isthmus of Panama, on July 13, 1868. He preached in Stockton until October when Bishop Marvin appointed him in charge of the Methodist Church in San Francisco. He served there for two years and seven months. While in San Francisco, he was engaged as principal editor of the *Spectator*. Wood then had an appointment to Vallejo and Napa. He gave notice to the Methodist conference that he did not agree with them "in matters of doctrine and church policy. . .and asked to withdraw, but was persuaded to remain a member." Wood chose to live in St. Helena, Napa County, where he taught school before an appointment to teach at Chico on October 22, 1871.[7]

At the October 1873 Pacific Annual Conference, the Reverend Jesse Wood, Pastor of the Methodist Episcopal Church South, was condemned for his political involvement by accepting a nomination for School Superintendent. At his request, he was granted a place in the conference. Following the conference, Wood and a group of influential citizens formed a new religious society called the Christian Union of Chicago.[8]

While preaching at Chico, Wood taught public school until May, 1876, when he became deputy county clerk and pastor of the First Congregational Church. He was appointed clerk in July, 1877, to fill an unexpired term. Three months later, Wood was elected superintendent of public schools, then elected again in 1879.[9] During his second term, he wrote the early history of Butte County Schools.[10]

Wood leased the voice of the Democratic party, the *Enterprise,* in 1883, and served as its editor for one year. By September 25, 1887, Jesse Wood purchased *The Chico Record.* He then consolidated it with the *Morning Chronicle.* Wood and two other men joined forces as owners and publishers and formed the Chico Publishing Company which, for approximately eight years, published *The Chico Chronicle-Record.*[11]

Jesse and Alice Wood lived with their family of ten children — six girls and four boys — at their homestead farm, "Eyrie Villa," in Oregon township. The farm was so named because of its elevation and beautiful view. Wood made a number of significant improvements to enhance the property. He was a well respected and active member of the community.[12]

Hazel always thought of her father warmly. She remembered how Jesse Wood had a strong interest in higher education. Even though the family had minimal income, he wanted to send all the children to the university. His philosophy was that a good education was an essential part of life. Because of her father, Hazel had a year at Berkeley and the advanced

Waldo Sprague Waterman (Bancroft Library).

training that helped sharpen her artistic eye for detail in design.[13] She was fortunate to meet someone like Waldo, a man from a similarly strong family background. The two were immediately compatible.

Waldo's father, Robert Whitney Waterman, seventeenth governor of California, was born on December 15, 1826, in Fairfield, New York. He was descended from early pioneers of the state.[14] His father, John Dean Waterman, had married Mary Graves Waldo on December 31, 1819. They were the parents of nine children — six boys and three girls.[18] Several years after his father died, Robert Waterman joined with his two older brothers in Newburg, Illinois, where they were involved in merchandising. By age twenty, Robert owned a general store in Belvidere, Illinois. The following year, 1847, he married Jane Gardner of the same town. He and Jane had two children. During this time, between 1849 and 1850, Robert Waterman served as postmaster at Geneva, Illinois.[16]

Waterman went to California in 1850, by ox team; there he joined his brother Theodore. Before opening a store near the Feather and Yuba Rivers, he mined for gold in the area. Waterman soon relocated with his family to Wilmington, Illinois, where from 1852 to 1860 he published the *Independent*. Waterman helped establish the Republican Party of Illinois. As a campaign supporter, he assisted Fremont and Dayton, and later Abraham Lincoln.[17]

The Watermans and their now seven children moved to Redwood City, California, via the transcontinental railroad in 1873. A year later, they settled in an area of San Bernardino which later became Waterman Canyon. Waterman and John C. Porter, a mining engineer, found a rich silver strike in 1880 near the Grapevine in the volcanic hills. The mine, in the Chico District, netted about $1,000,000 in profit between 1881 and 1887. After the value of silver dropped, the mine closed.

Waterman built a mill near the mine, the Southern Pacific Railroad, Mojave-Needles right-of-way and the Mojave River. Waterman Junction resulted and became Barstow in 1886.[18]

On July 23, 1884, at the Republican State Convention, Waterman was elected as an alternate elector at large. He received the nomination and was elected Lieutenant Governor in 1887. He served in that capacity for eight months until Governor Washington Bartlett died. Waterman became governor on September 13, 1887. After the inauguration, Governor Waterman said: "I intend to run the office of Governor as I would my private business. There are two things I will never tolerate, dishonesty and drunkenness." The *Sacramento Union* described Waterman as a "lover of fair play" and felt he would not be subservient to bosses or cliques.[19]

Governor Waterman was known for diligence in routine matters and detailed consideration of legislative bills. His state duties were numerous. He was an ex-officio member of the board of examiners and

> In reference to his own office, Waterman said: 'the Governor, besides the duties that demand his attention at the Capitol, is the President of the State Board of Education, the President of the Board of Regents of the State University, the President of the three Boards of Normal School Trustees, the Chairman of the Yosemite Commissioners, and the Chairman of the State Board of Capitol Commissioners and it is further made obligatory upon him as Chief Executive to visit, as often as possible, the different prisons, asylums, and other institutions of the state.'[20]

After visiting the state institutions, Governor Waterman became interested in having the San Quentin prison become self-supporting. Provisions made by the legislature of 1889-1890 for a dam and canal at Folsom Prison which would use the water power from the American River were nearly completed. He gave much consideration to irrigation district problems and

Hazel W. Waterman as a young woman (Bancroft Library).

utilized the Wright Act of 1887 approved by Governor Bartlett. In addition, during his term, a homesite for feeble-minded children at Glen Ellin was selected, reformatories at Whittier and Ione and more insane asylums at San Bernardino and Ukiah were established.[21]

Governor Waterman criticized an attempt to divide the state by saying: "There is and can be but one California." He also censured legislative extravagance. Waterman stated that as governor, he was the first to place the state on "a cash paying basis." California had been in arrears since 1877, yet "At the end of his administration the total funded indebtedness still amounted to $2,642,000, and he recommended a refunding of this debt."[22]

Waterman maintained that the University of California, where his son Waldo was graduated in 1886, was the "only absolutely free University in the world with its academic departments." Although a friend of education, he pocket vetoed a county high school bill that had been passed by the legislature in 1889 to assist schools in preparing students for entrance to the university. Because of the previous administration's legislation however, the Chico State Normal School, in Jesse Wood's area, began operations. Waterman nevertheless lost support toward the end of his term and created ill will when he exercised his prerogatives and made full use of his pardoning ability. Although considered, Waterman did not receive renomination. The governor's "strongest trait was integrity and he was nicknamed 'Old Honesty'."[23]

Robert Whitney Waterman (Bancroft Library).

Notes
Chapter One

[1]Family Record, Waterman Line, 1758-1930. Typescript, San Diego Historical Society Research Archives, San Diego, California, hereinafter referred to as SDHSRA.

[2]*Ibid.* Waldo D. Waterman interview with Mary Jessop, January 25, 1970, pp. 9, 14; Typescript, SDHSRA; Waldo D. Waterman interview with Mary F. Ward, January 14, 1971, pp. 1, 2; Typescript, SDHSRA. Waldo Dean Waterman, born June 16, 1894, was the second son, youngest child of Hazel Wood Waterman and Waldo Sprague Waterman, letter from Waldo Waterman to Jane Waterman, October 24, 1888.

[3]University of California, *Yearbook,* 1886, The Bancroft Library.

[4]Family Record, Waterman Line, 1758-1930, Typescript, SDHSRA. Harry L. Wells and W.L. Chambers, *History of Butte County, California,* 2 vols. in 1 (San Francisco: Harry L. Wells, 1882), pp. 304, 305; Sarah W. Spiess, "Hazel Waterman, Architect of the Wednesday Club," February 1979, p. 2 Typescript Wednesday Club Archives; Waldo D. Waterman interview with Mary F. Ward, January 14, 1971, p. 1, Typescript, SDHSRA.

[5]Wells and Chambers, *History of Butte County;* John Waterland, "Pioneer Activities," *Chico Record,* July 7, 1935, indicates that he graduated from the Southern University of Alabama.

[6]Wells and Chambers, *History of Butte County,* pp. 304-305.

[7]*Ibid.*

[8]Waterland, *Chico Record,* July 7, 1935.

[9]Wells and Chambers, *History of Butte County,* p. 305.

[10]Waterland, *Chico Record,* July 12, 1936.

[11]*Ibid.,* May 17, 1936.

[12]Wells and Chambers, *History of Butte County,* p. 305.

[13]Waldo D. Waterman interview with Mary F. Ward, January 14, 1971, pp. 1, 2. Typescript, SDHSRA.

[14]H. Brett Melendy and Benjamin F. Gilbert, *The Governors of California* (Georgetown, California: The Talisman Press, 1965), p. 227.

[15]The Waterman Line, SDHSRA.

[16]Melendy and Gilbert, *Governors,* p. 227.

[17]*Ibid.*

[18]*Ibid.,* pp. 227, 228.

[19]*Ibid.,* p. 230.

[20]*Ibid.,* pp. 230-231.

[21]*Ibid.,* pp. 231, 233, 234.

[22]*Ibid.,* pp. 231-232.

[23]*Ibid.*

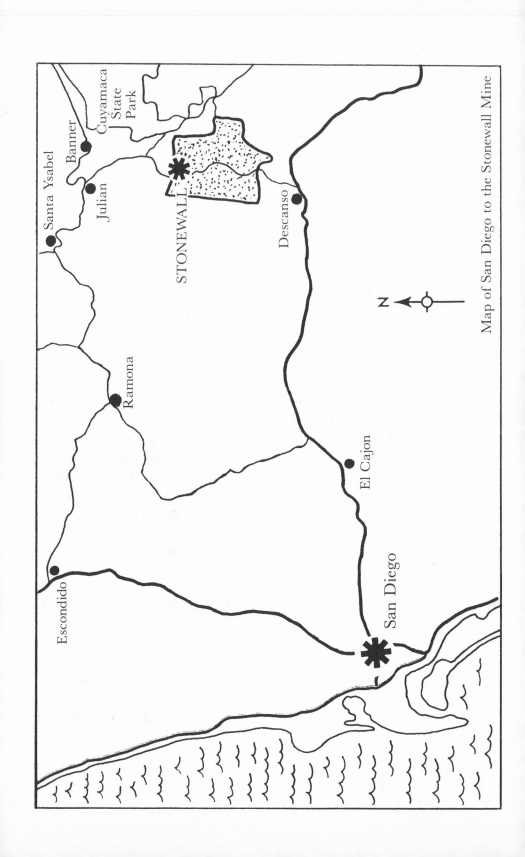

Map of San Diego to the Stonewall Mine

Chapter Two
The Julian-Cuyamaca Years

BECAUSE WALDO'S FATHER had purchased the Stonewall mine in Southern California, and Waldo had recently received training as a mining engineer, the young Watermans moved to the Julian Consolidated Mining District shortly after their marriage. When Hazel and Waldo arrived at the mine, they found that many changes had occurred in the mining area since the five cousins, two Julian brothers and three Bailey brothers, from a little town in Georgia, arrived on the first of November, 1869. They could see the distant Volcan Mountain in the north, the Palomar toward the northwest, the Cuyamacas to the south.[1] Although not visible, they knew the Pacific Ocean was in the west and the desert in the east.[2]

The development of the Julian district was of great importance to Hazel and Waldo, since they would be making a home in the area. Its American settlement actually began with the arrival of the Horral, Brady and Webb families, the first in the area from the mid-west, who had preceded the Julians and Baileys by about three years. Drury (Drue) Bailey decided to homestead the land which is now the town of Julian. The cousins staked off their land claims, then proceeded to build a cabin at the southern end of the valley. Drue selected the land at the head of the valley, where the town of Julian now stands, to plant his barley.[3]

Soon gold discoveries began to occur. Mike Julian found a nugget while he panned a creek in a draw near the cabin. Later this became the Helvetia mine and Swytzer Flats. Then in the middle of December, 1869, in a creek now known as

Coleman's, four miles west of the cabin, two men, Woods and Coleman found placer. While prospecting for quartz one mile north of the cabin, Putnam and Hammel found ore and located the Van Wirt mine.[4]

On the following day, February 21, 1870, Bickers, Wills and Gower found a quartz ledge which became the Washington mine. Drue Bailey tried his luck. He met with success in March when he found the San Diego and Good Hope mines. Some of the others that followed included the Owens, High Peak, Eagle, Helvetia, and the California.[5] Also in March, William Skidmore located the Stonewall Jackson Mine near the Cuyamaca Lake and began operations after the erection of a stamp mill. By May, Almon P. Frary purchased the mine.[6]

Foresighted Drue Bailey realized the need for a business center. He hired a surveyor to plot a section of his property closest to the mining center. Drue then named that townsite after his popular cousin, Mike Julian. Mike had been elected recorder on February 15, 1870, after the concerned, early arrivals decided to form the Julian Mining District and adopt by-laws to protect their interests. Later the mining district and the first school district were named after him. They also elected him as a trustee of the Board.[7]

Another historic event to have a major effect on the young Watermans was the granting of the Cuyamaca Rancho into private ownership in 1845. In that year, Governor Pio Pico granted one of Southern California's last ranchos, 35,501 acres of mountain timber land, to Agustin Olvera. Five years later, the United States Land Commission rejected Olvera's claim for a patent. He had failed to comply with the patent requirements of boundary descriptions and maps which showed the location of his rancho in San Diego County. After Olvera appealed, he regained title when the California District Court confirmed his grant in 1858. The government failed in an

20-Stamp Mill at Stonewall Mine (Bancroft Library).

31

attempt to appeal the case since it missed the final deadline for recourse.[8]

Four men, Robert Allison, Isaac Hartman, Juan Luco and John Treat, bought the Cuyamaca Rancho in 1869, from Olvera. With the discovery of gold, their rancho boundaries conveniently moved northward to encompass the total Julian mining district. By the following spring, they informed the more than 500 miners who had moved into the area that a royalty had to be paid on all ore if they intended to continue to work their claims. Miners figured that the schedule of royalties, issued by the owners, combined with the milling costs, would leave them with less than half their usual profit.[9]

This upset generated public interest when the indignant miners refused to work and cancelled their machinery orders.[10] Within about two weeks, on June 9, the land grant owners engaged James Pasco to conduct a survey, "not according to the terms of the grant or the description of the diseño, but in a manner which they requested."[11] The surveyor's report supported the owners' contention that the boundaries included the mining camps of Julian, Banner, and Stonewall.[12] In retaliation, the miners created a Defense League, and retained a lawyer to fight their case in court.[13]

The costly land battle continued for several years. Beginning in June 1871, the United States Surveyor General ruled in the League's favor. Then later the following year, in Washington, D.C., the Land Commission reviewed the case and remanded it to the United States Surveyor General. The League won the case at the end of November 1873. The final ruling indicated that the land grant proved invalid since Governor Pio Pico failed to sign the original deed. In the end, the re-surveyed land, which set new boundaries, was returned to the miners.[14]

The ton of ore taken to San Diego and San Francisco for

exhibition created great excitement, though not of the same magnitude the forty-niners in the north had experienced. Yet the word spread and people began to move toward the remote new mining district in Southern California, San Diego's back country, to seek their fortunes. A major obstacle, however, was the lack of roads impeding travel to and from the town. The cost was high to pack in supplies over the first and only trail. "The old Kanaka Trail . . . came in from Temecula, past the Santa Ysabel Mission, up the draws past the homes of the first three settlers at the foot of Volcan Mountain." A toll road constructed from Santa Ysabel, down through Spencer Valley and then to Julian, became a public highway when purchased later by the county.[15]

As travel conditions improved, a regular mail, four-horse stageline ran between San Diego and Julian. Wells Fargo Express opened an office in Julian.[16] Heavy freight wagons hauled gold ore to San Diego, then it went on to a smelter near San Francisco and finally to the mint and banks in San Francisco.

The banks in San Diego and other areas never submitted figures as to the value of the amounts deposited. Estimates of production amounts have varied between $5,000,000 and as high as $13,000,000.[17] Generally the estimated figure, although considered quite conservative, from the most reliable sources, remains comfortable at around $5,000,000. "Much unrecorded gold was shipped out of Julian and never went through the mint."[18] There were no restrictions on the sale of gold in those early days before the Franklin Roosevelt administration. The demand for the very high grade — 940 to 970 fine — Julian gold came from banks, smelters, jewelers and dental companies. They purchased thousands of dollars worth directly from the miners. Even the Empress of China obtained hundreds of bars of gold.[19] Reports also indicated that what had seemed to be rich leads were only pockets caused by a shifting of the earth

The Long-Waterman House, San Diego, San Diego (San Diego Historical Society).

which pinched out the veins of ore. "A shifting of the rock mass caused the layers of quartz to move sometimes more than a mile from their original position.[20] Thus, the miner following a rich vein one day might well come up against a blank wall with no inkling as to which way the rock had shifted. Fortunately, in the early days of mining, much of the richest ore was found at or near the surface and was free milling. At greater depths they often ran into sulphides which caused the closing of the mines, since at that time the miners had not the equipment for recovering gold from this ore."[21] Only the Watermans' mine, the Stonewall, remained free from the faulting and other problems miners encountered elsewhere. Away from the fault zone, the mine veins proved to be stable as in the case of the Stonewall. Eventually only internal flooding caused it to close.[22]

Waldo had been hired by his father, Robert Whitney Waterman, to manage the Stonewall Mine.[23] The governor purchased the mine after he visited Julian in the fall of 1886. Conflicting sources give the purchase price as $45,000 or $75,000.[24] Shortly afterwards, with the press of his business and political duties, he needed Waldo to help with the extensive improvements necessary to operate the mine profitably. With Waldo's assistance, Robert Waterman spent more than $50,000 to improve the conditions of the Stonewall operation.[25]

Robert Waterman also purchased, in addition to the mine's seven acres referred to as Lot A, 26,000 acres of Cuyamaca Land Grant that gave him control of all the mining and mill area. At that time, the 10-stamp mill at the mine had a capacity of about 20 tons per 24 hours. Before Waldo Waterman began his new role as superintendent, the mine shaft had several levels and had been deepened to 155 feet. One of Waldo's most significant tasks was to sink a second shaft southeast of the first. Soon the shaft was 400 feet deep and finally it became the deepest in the area with a depth of more than 600 feet. The installation of a $100,000 20-stamp mill in February of 1889,

Employees at Stonewall Mine (Bancroft Library).

Stonewall Mine Shed. The group of three persons on the right may be (left to right) Robert Waterman, his wife and Hazel Wood Waterman. (San Diego Historical Society).

increased the ore crushing capacity to 90 tons per day and production stepped up to even greater proportions. Between 1888
and 1891, the Stonewall operation shipped over $900,000 worth
of gold.[26] By 1893, nearly two million dollars in gold had been
removed from the mine. "Total final production from the Julian
Banner mines probably reached between $4,000,000 and
$5,000,000."[27]

To prevent the possibility of hold-ups when gold was
transported to San Diego, Governor Waterman preferred to
avoid regular shipments by public carrier such as Wells Fargo.
Of the several plans devised,

> one was to send a light wagon with a team of fast horses and an armed
> guard dashing down the mountain, supposedly with a shipment of
> gold, while behind came a lumbering freight wagon actually hauling
> the bullion, which stopped overnight in Alpine, where the gold was
> stored in the safe of the Alpine Store. The next day they continued
> their leisurely pace down the mountain.[28]

The tremendous production demands created the need
for more mine and sawmill workers. As the men who sought
employment arrived with their families, a little town called
Cuyamaca City sprang up in the area which surrounded the
mine and the southeastern shore of the lake. As needs arose,
various businesses began to appear. Soon there was a general
store, a two-story hotel, post office, bunk house for the single
men, a few houses for those with families and a school. Governor Waterman constructed the sawmill which provided lumber
to extend the mine and erect buildings.[29]

With the influx of miners, and the lack of recreational
facilities at the mine, fights broke out with frequency particularly among German and Irish workers. The management
became concerned about their inability to work because of
severe injuries when the men used their fists, clubs or anything
available to beat up one another. The superintendent purchased
books, checkers, dominos, games and a phonograph with

cylinder records. The regrettable selection of the record, "It Takes the Irish To Beat The Dutch," ended in the most brutal fight of all which ruined the room and wrecked the phonograph.[30]

During this period, Governor Waterman traveled to San Diego frequently. On the occasion of one of his visits, Jesse Shepard held a reception in honor of the governor at his stately Victorian home, the Villa Montezuma, located at 20th and K Streets.[31] Governor Waterman left a week later with Waldo for the Julian mine.

Notes
Chapter Two

[1]Helen Ellsberg, *Mines of Julian* (Glendale, California: La Siesta Press, 1972), p. 1; *History of Julian,* 1964, p. 3 (the year refers to the incorporation date of the Julian Historical Society; there were numerous contributors).

[2]*History of Julian,* p. 1.

[3]*Ibid.,* p. 3.

[4]*Ibid.,* p. 4.

[5]*Ibid.,* p. 5.

[6]Ellsberg, *Mines of Julian,* p. 34.

[7]Dan Forrest Taylor, "Julian Gold," F.E.C. Federal Writers' Project, San Diego, California, Feb. 8, 1939, pp. 22, 26. Typescript, SDHSRA.

[8]Ellsberg, *Mines of Julian,* p. 19; Cecil Moyer, *Historic Ranchos of San Diego,* ed. by Richard F. Pourade (San Diego, California: Union-Tribune Publishing Company, 1969), p. 78; Olvera was an early resident of Los Angeles, for whom Olvera Street is named.

[9]Ellsberg, *Mines of Julian,* p. 19; Moyer, *Historic Ranchos,* p. 79.

[10]Ellsberg, *Mines of Julian,* p. 19.

[11]*Ibid.,* p. 21.

[12]*History of Julian,* p. 12.

[13]Ellsberg, *Mines of Julian,* p. 21.

[14]*History of Julian,* p. 13; Moyer, *Historic Ranchos,* p. 79.

[15]*History of Julian,* p. 5.

[16]*Ibid.,* pp. 5, 8.

[17]Ellsberg, *Mines of Julian,* p. 10; *History of Julian,* p. 12.

[18]Ellsberg, *Mines of Julian,* p. 10.

[19]*Ibid.* In 1873, Rossiter W. Raymond explained in an annual report that prejudice against the miners was the reason for the slow development of the mines in Southern California. Resentment caused derogatory mine reports to be sent to capitalists in San Francisco. Lengthy litigation of the Cuyamaca Land Grant battle, and the Civil War animosities against the large number of southerners who had settled in the area, created distrust among potential northern investors who harbored strong feelings against the largely Confederate-owned mines in the Julian Banner district.

[20]Ellsberg, *Mines of Julian,* pp. 8, 9. To further complicate the erratic behavior of the veins, the formation is split by fault lines, primarily the Elsinore fault which cuts the eastern end of the area in Banner and Rodrigues canyons and the Agua Tibia Fault whose course from the northeast end of Volcan Mountain, through Warners, and on down into Baja California, is marked by hot sulphur springs.

[21]Ellsberg, *Mines of Julian,* pp. 11, 13.

[22]*Ibid.,* p. 13

[23]Waldo D. Waterman interview with Mary F. Ward, January 14, 1971, p. 2. Typescript, SDHSRA; Taylor, "Julian Gold," Febuary 8, 1939, pp. 4, 5. Typescript, SDHSRA.

[24]*Ibid.,* Ellsberg, *Mines of Julian,* p. 35.

[25]Taylor, "Julian Gold," pp, 22, 25.

[26]Ellsberg, *Mines of Julian,* p. 35; *History of Julian,* p. 18.

[27]Moyer, *Historic Ranchos,* p. 81.

[28]Ellsberg, *Mines of Julian,* p. 37.

[29]*History of Julian,* p. 18.

[30]Ellsberg, *Mines of Julian,* p. 35, 37.

[31]Handwritten note, June 22, 1888, The Bancroft Library, Waterman Collection. The Villa Montezuma is presently operated by the San Diego Historical Society as a museum and cultural center.

Mining Works, Stonewall Mine (San Diego Historical Society).

Chapter Three
Daily Life in the Mining Region

Hazel ADJUSTED TO the primitive living conditions in the Cuyamaca area even though her earlier days had not prepared her for life in a remote mining camp. Although life in Julian proved to be difficult, Hazel took advantage of spare moments to develop her landscape painting technique. During the years spent at Cuyamaca, she drew sketches and painted pictures of the beautiful back country. Her first born, Robert Wood Waterman, arrived in the remote mountain area the day after Christmas, 1889. Even though the winter was severely cold, Hazel recovered quickly and the Watermans enjoyed their new son. Just six months later, Hazel became pregnant again and experienced some difficult times. Helen Gardner Waterman, was born on March 7, 1891.[1]

Tragedy struck the Waterman family on April 12, 1981, when Hazel's father-in-law, former Governor Robert Waterman, died unexpectedly at sixty-five.[2] The pressure of his state duties coupled with the multiplicity of his business activities had taken its toll. He had been working to develop the mine's potential by bringing in special machinery and making extensive improvements.[3]

Two years before his death, in 1889, Governor Waterman authorized E.F. Spence to sell the 21,000 acre Rancho Cuyamaca, the Stonewall Mine and everything pertaining thereto, the Saw Mill and all teams, wagons, horses, mules and cattle which were estimated at between five hundred and a thousand head. Spence had an exclusive for six months with a commission of fifty thousand dollars. Unfortunately, Spence failed to make a deal.[4] The governor had suffered many times from the cold, but unable to unload the mines and other properties, continued to spend much of his time in the Cuyamaca-Julian area. His son Waldo had complained of his own physical problems during that time to his mother, emphasizing that the severe winters at the mine caused him to be sick with rheumatism, recurring colds and a malaria flare up. Hazel also confided to Mother Waterman of the hard winters at Cuyamaca. When the governor was in Sacramento, Waldo wrote frequently to him to keep him informed about troubles with the mine's water pump, the lack of quality ore, and the poor rock.[5]

The Spence exclusive ran out in August of 1890. Governor Waterman seemed to have a sense of urgency when he entered into an agreement with Robert Gardner to purchase seven mines — Desert View, Mountain Brow, Mamouth, Gardner, Richmond, Compromise, and Julian — and the Hastings Mill Site, all for fifty thousand dollars.[6] The sale was never consumated. To step up production and increase revenue, Waldo urged that a new stamp mill and more cattle be purchased. Soon installed, the new stamp mill seemed to be the answer to obtaining more and higher quality ore. Then trouble began with a mine cave-in at the fourth level. Waldo found it difficult to get and keep good men. He complained of being short handed.[7]

To keep up with the financial demands of his many business holdings, Governor Waterman attempted to establish a line of credit with the Consolidated National Bank of San Diego. On September 22, 1890, he signed "written obligations or 'promissory notes' as security for" a loan of $91,366 plus interest in the sum of $9,145.03. All debts were due on December 17, 1891 and to be paid in "gold coin of the United States."[8]

Hazel was going through her second pregnancy during this time. She experienced anxiety over the inability to keep adequate help. She had to replace the nurse and cook and objected to the boarding house conditions. A new nurse, a frail little English girl of thirty with the name of Miss Comfort, arrived in early November and a former cook returned so pressures were somewhat lessened.[9] Because of the closeness of her pregnancies, Hazel became weakened and quite nervous while in the middle and late months. Waldo's married sister, Anna Charlotte Waterman Scott, stayed at Cuyamaca to help Hazel through her confinement period. Anna urged Waldo to hire a new nurse to assist with procedures two months before the baby was due.[10] The eight pound baby girl, Helen Gardner Waterman, arrived without incident on March 7, 1891.[11]

By early March 1891, Waldo again alerted his father over the concern for the poor quality rock the mine produced. Because their luck appeared to be "running out,"[12] the Governor decided to visit the mine to determine the full extent of the problems that existed. While there, he became ill and returned to San Diego. The heavy schedule, worry and lack of sleep, left him unable to fight off the simple cold which led to pneumonia and death at his home at 2408 First Street.[13]

The death of Governor Waterman came as a shock to all who knew him. Letters of condolence came from all parts of the state.[14] According to the newspapers, his estate was estimated at eight million dollars. Probate records, however, indicate that the actual amount was considerably less.[15] Waterman's term as California Governor had ended on January 15, 1891, and he was finally able to devote himself to his business interests.

In addition to his mining activities, Robert Waterman had always been interested in railroad transportation. After he became President of the Board of the San Diego, Cuyamaca and Eastern Railroad Company, on March 11, 1889.[16] Governor Waterman began to build a railroad that would run from San Diego to Yuma. The line used borrowed rolling equipment from the Coronado, National City & Otay and Southern

Pacific railroads to run "from Ninth and Commercial Streets in San Diego, through Lemon Grove, La Mesa . . ." and Lakeside to Foster. Every day, four-horse stages met two trains to provide direct service to the Julian and Banner mining districts which had been combined.[17] Waterman intended to open the route to the east by going through Yuma instead of Los Angeles. He also planned that the line would serve the mine by going over the mountains to Ramona and Julian ". . . but expenses and mountains stood in the way."[18] Unfortunately, construction reached only as far as the little town of Foster, located "at the upper end of the El Cajon Valley, twenty-five miles northeast of San Diego, and thirty-six miles from Julian," before Robert Waterman passed away.[19]

Other problems involving the mine operations constantly plagued the company. The City of San Diego wanted to acquire Waterman's land and expand the dam that provided water for the vast agricultural area in the Lakeside-Spring section of the county. They planned to buy the land and expand the reservoir to make it the major source of water for the city. Robert Waterman resisted their attempts to make the purchase since he believed that increased water in the area would contribute to the nearly uncontrollable flooding within the mine. Waterman had already purchased and brought in a pump from San Francisco capable of removing 400 gallons of water per minute to stay ahead of the 100 gallons of water per minute that gushed into the mine.[20]

The city then filed a successful condemnation suit against the mining company since the public need required more water. The governor appealed the suit, and the court compromised by awarding him some cash, other lands, and a reversionary clause that enabled him or his estate to take back the land if the city discontinued its use of the area as a reservoir. Despite Waterman's efforts, the dam ruined the mine by making it unworkable. The large pumps could not economically keep the excessive amount of water from flowing into the mine. This forced the formerly rich Stonewall Mine to close following the death of Robert Waterman.[21]

Later, the property was taken over by the Sather Banking Co. of San Francisco who had the mine tailings processed. Then in 1917, Col. A.G. Glassen purchased the Cuyamaca Rancho, which included the Waterman property and mine. Within six years, he sold the acreage to Ralph M. Dyar, who built a sizable stone ranchhouse on the land. In time, a Los Angeles wrecking company bought the buildings for scrap. The old relics and ore cars were pushed down into the mine's open shaft. The State of California purchased 20,735 acres of the Rancho in 1933 for nearly $125,000 "—half of the assessed valuation of the land—. . .".[22]

Hazel Waterman's major role, while in residence at the mine, centered on her home and her husband's activities. During their first winter at the mine after the Governor's passing, Hazel wrote to Mother Waterman about the "wind, snow and bitter cold." She told how the children suffered and cried often from continuous bad colds. Despite the many illnesses, she tried to make the best of it. She was able to visit San Diego once in awhile and take advantage of the warmer climate.[23] Hazel cheerfully talked about how well "I manage to get the work done," and "how domestic and lovely Waldo is." Hazel now began to establish her own identity which was reflected when she signed her letters for the first time as, Hazel Wood Waterman.[24]

Waldo faced the mining and other problems squarely, even though he lacked his father's business experience. Unfortunately, he now had to deal with numerous promissory notes that were called in when the Waterman business ventures went sour.[25] Named executrix of the estate, mother Jane G. Waterman was immediately responsible to her sons James and Waldo, and daughters Mary, Helen, Abbie and Anna. Mother Waterman was only sixty-one years old, yet her handwriting appeared very shaky which may indicate she did not enjoy good health.[26]

As an unusually conservative and perhaps ill-advised move, Jane Waterman took out five separate insurance policies on the Stonewall Mine, the buildings and machinery. Each policy was with a different company for the same amount of twenty-four thousand dollars which made a total of $120,000. By the following year, Sather Banking Company sued Jane G. Waterman for $124,090.44 which included interest and costs. Once again Mother Waterman took out insurance. This time the policy covered her San Diego home, and stable buildings in the rear, at First and Kalmia Streets. On November 9, 1892, Waldo's brother James gave him his Power of Attorney. This vote of confidence by James influenced Mother Waterman to give Waldo her Power of Attorney and proxy votes. The Watermans were forced to take out several mortgages on their property holdings and cattle with different banks in San Diego and San Bernardino. Mother Waterman mortgaged their Bay View lots for a ten thousand dollar par value with the Savings Bank of San Diego. Much to her disappointment, the mortgage was later cancelled.[27]

Notes
Chapter Three

[1]Waldo D. Waterman interview with Mary F. Ward, January 14, 1971, pp. 1, 2. Typescript, SDHSRA; Family Record, Waterman Line, 1758-1930. Typescript SDHSRA.

[2]Certified Copy of Death Record, Robert Whitney Waterman, San Diego, April 12, 1891. County Recorders Office, County Administration Building. Family Record, Waterman Line, 1758-1930. SDHSRA. Dan Forrest Taylor, "Julian Gold," February 8, 1939, p. 26. Typescript, SDHSRA.

[3]Taylor, "Julian Gold," p. 25.

[4]The Bancroft Library, Waterman Collection, R.W. Waterman to E.F. Spence, San Diego, 1889.

[5]The Bancroft Library, Waterman Collection, Waldo Waterman to mother (Jane Waterman) October 2, 1888.

[6]The Bancroft Library, Waterman Collection, Agreement, Robert W. Waterman with Robert Gardner, San Diego, August 2, 1890.

[7]The Bancroft Library, Waterman Collection, Waldo Waterman to Robert Waterman, September 9, 1890, and October 19, 1890, Cuyamaca.

[8]The Bancroft Library, Waterman Collection, Promissory Notes, September 22, 1890, San Diego, R.W. Waterman.

[9]The Bancroft Library, Waterman Collection, Hazel to Jane Waterman, Cuyamaca, November 5, 1890.

[10]The Bancroft Library, Waterman Collection, Anna Charlotte Waterman to "Girls" (Helen and Abby) Cuyamaca, December 21, 1890 and January 4, 1891.

[11]The Bancroft Library, Waterman Collection, Waldo Waterman, Cuyamaca, March 7, 1891 to Robert W. Waterman.

[12]The Bancroft Library, Waldo W. to RWW, Cuyamaca, March 9, 1891.

[13]Obituary, R.W. Waterman, April 13, 1891, San Francisco Examiner; see also Karen Johl, *Timeless Treasures: San Diego's Victorian Heritage* (San Diego: Rand Editions, 1982), which has a picture of the Long-Waterman house on cover. The Watermans purchased the Victorian home in 1891 for $17,000.00.

[14]The Bancroft Library, Waterman Collection.

[15]In the Matter of the Estate of Robert Waterman, Superior Court of San Diego County, No. 775, Department Two.

[16]The Bancroft Library, Waterman Collection, Minutes of the San Diego, Cuyamaca and Eastern Railroad, March 11, 1889.

[17]Richard F. Pourade, *The Glory Years* (San Diego, California: The Union Tribune Publishing Company, 1969), p. 231.

[18]Waldo D. Waterman interview with Mary Jessop, January 25, 1970, pp. 10, 11. Typescript SDHSRA.

[19]A note in the Bancroft Library indicated that from January 1st to 16th inclusive, the SDC & E RR had earned $895.55 from passengers, $685.59 from freight, and $17.18 from mail, or a total of $1,598.32; Taylor, "Julian Gold," February 8, 1939, p. 25. Typescript, SDHSRA.

[20]Waldo D. Waterman interview with Mary Jessop, January 25, 1970, p. 11, 12. Typescript, SDHSRA.

[21]*Ibid.,* Waldo D. Waterman interview with Mary Jessop, January 25, 1970, pp. 11, 12. Typescript, SDHSRA.

[22]Moyer, *Historic Ranchos,* p. 81.

[23]The Bancroft Library, Waterman Collection, Hazel Waterman to Helen Waterman, San Diego, November 19, 1891.

[24]The Bancroft Library, Waterman Collection, Cuyamaca, Hazel Waterman to Jane Waterman, February 1, 1892.

[25]Waldo D. Waterman interview with Mary Jessop, January 25, 1970, p. 12. Typescript SDHSRA.

[26]The Bancroft Library, letter from Jane Waterman, San Diego, California (no date). The heirs of the Waterman Estate were James S., Waldo S., Mary P. (Waterman) Rice, Helen J. Abbie L. and Annie C.

[27]The Bancroft Library, Jane Waterman to Savings Bank, December, 1892.

"Granite Cottage," designed for Hazel & Waldo Waterman by Irving Gill (San Diego Historical Society).

Chapter Four
The Watermans in San Diego

Although economic progress continued in San Diego, the boom of the 1880s had passed. The 1890s brought hard times to many people. After five San Diego banks failed in 1893, only three, the San Diego Savings Bank, Bank of Commerce and the First National Bank remained open.[1] This had a direct effect on the Watermans' finances. The Consolidated National Bank, that had held the Waterman Railroad bonds as collateral, closed and was "unable to honor a five hundred dollar check written by Stonewall Mine, Waldo S. Waterman, Manager." Waldo wrote to his mother about the bad news. "I wired you today of the closing of the two principal banks here. This has been to me an awful day."[2]

The Waterman estate nearly entered bankruptcy when the mine and the Cuyamaca land holdings were liquidated. Little remained in the estate after the promissory notes were paid off, except the railroad that led to nowhere, a small portion of land, and an unprofitable silver mine in Barstow, California [3] near the ranch where the governor had once raised pedigreed cattle.[4]

Waldo had the task of running a railroad and producing sufficient funds to support his family. In the fall of 1893, the pressure of Waldo's responsibilities increased when he learned that Hazel expected another child. With his wife's encouragement, Waldo moved the family to San Diego so they could have their third baby in the city. Hazel wanted their children to have the benefits of more modern conveniences and the local school system. Waldo rented the Monteit house on Third Street above

Walnut just before their second son, Waldo Dean Waterman arrived on June 16, 1894. Hazel wrote to Mother Waterman that she had twins, but that the baby girl never breathed.[5]

In conjunction with Waldo's railroad activities, he managed to secure a contract for harbor development. The contract stated he would "furnish and deliver brush, loaded on board cars at Wells Station on the Coronado Railroad in San Diego County, for building of Jetty and Jetty Works at mouth of San Diego Bay. $2.75 per cord."[6] With other opportunities such as this, Waldo became more confident about the future of the railroad. He said, "The prospects for a good year were never better. We have $5,000 in the bank and hope to increase that right along."[7]

Hazel told Mother Waterman of Waldo's new feeling of optimism, which led him to participate in the 1894 Cabrillo Celebration Parade.[8] Hazel and the children enjoyed watching him drive past with the other dignitaries. This was a pleasant time for the Waterman family even though Waldo was experiencing problems in business.[9]

Hazel gave insight to their personal finances when she indicated they were unable to save money. They had moved into an older house that proved to be in poor condition. She said it was expensive to "fix over" and that many of their "own things are old and shabby." She hoped "to get a cheaper girl, the last one left without notice. I wish I could get along without anybody, but the two children and nursing baby are too much and I hire no serving done." To cut down expenses and minimize her domestic demands, Hazel remade Waldo's clothes for their elder son Robert. She kept her only daughter Helen "in overalls to save washing."[10] Nevertheless, life was not difficult for Hazel. She lived in pleasant surroundings and was able to visit relatives in San Francisco from time to time. Apparently son Robert had suffered from an illness and was seeing a doctor in San Francisco. Hazel reported that "Robert grows stronger, has a good appetite . . . is going to doctor Friday."[11]

As Hazel and Waldo developed friendships within the community, they found themselves attracted to those of similar backgrounds who were interested in a more scholarly type of social recreation. The Watermans were among the original members of the College Graduate Club which was formed on October 8, 1896, "to bring together persons with academic degrees to discuss at regular monthly meetings, current topics of the day."[12] Just past the turn of the century, topics for discussion became more controversial in nature. Waldo gave a talk on "Municipality Ownership or National Ownership of National Monopolies." Hazel's first talk focused on "Organized Labor," while later in 1905, she spoke on her advocacy of "the proposition that men under forty had accomplished practically all the valuable work of the world."[13]

By May, 1906, after the original strength and enthusiasm of the members had dwindled, the organization "changed its name to the University Club hoping to attract new members."[14] A reorganization occurred in late 1907, and by 1909, the Articles of Incorporation indicated the exclusion of women from the membership.[15] This caused Hazel to concentrate her intellect elsewhere.

For a while, Waldo failed to provide an adequate income. When the Watermans were unable to pay their rent, the bank evicted them and they were forced to move again. This time they rented a house on Second Street, between Fir and Date, where Waldo gradually accumulated some capital so that he could purchase land on which to build a home. He chose the northwest corner of Hawthorn and Albatross.[16]

Hazel and Waldo then selected and commissioned the talented young, thirty-year-old Irving Gill, whose architectural influence was widespread, as the architect to build their house.[17] Gill's talent enabled him to design neat and sanitary housing for Native Americans and low-income farm workers in addition to public buildings and large residences. "His idealistic concern for craftsmanship and art, and his humanistic concern for people set his buildings apart from all others."[18] This might have been why Hazel and Waldo Waterman were so intellectually attracted to Gill's design philosophies.

The house that Irving Gill

> . . . designed for Waldo and Hazel Waterman has a typically English feeling with its half-timbered gables and rough-hewn granite walls. Gill's touch is evident in the interiors where he tried to simplify housework by making door frames, chair rail and baseboards flush with plaster so that the beauty of woodwork was not marred by drudgery of dust.[19]

Hazel worked very closely with Gill, who was impressed by her instinctive understanding of architectural concepts. He seemed equally struck by Hazel's creativity, taste and individualism that influenced the design of the house during its construction.[20] Hazel had very definite ideas as to what she wanted in a home. Under her guidance, Gill designed the entrance and the kitchen so that they were deliberately placed to face the north. This would maximize the ability to have the bedrooms, living rooms and the south porch veranda look to the warmer south side. The efficient, oblong shaped kitchen shortened the distance between the sink, serving table and range. The north side windows and ventilating flue provided good air circulation. Hazel selected a gray granite of excellent quality from local quarries. "It is put together as roughly as I could persuade the masons to do it, with little mortar showing." She wanted the vines to cling to the granite and "the long line of the green roof." Hazel felt that "in a small house, one's rooms should all be rooms to 'live in'."[21] Gill often suggested to Hazel that if ever the situation might arise that she would want to earn a living, she should give serious thought to the

Irving Gill (San Diego Historical Society).

study of architecture. He felt Hazel Waterman had greater
ability and comprehension than any other clients.[22]

Stimulated by Irving Gill's association and encouragement, Hazel put her ideas on paper. She wrote an article on
their new home, "A Granite Cottage in California," which
appeared in the March 1902 issue of *The House Beautiful*. Hazel
discussed her architectural philosophy of the interior design
of their home stressing the extreme importance of functionalism
and the great need " . . . to economize steps, care, and labor
in all domestic affairs."[23] She expressed her personal feelings
saying:

> . . . I feel that ours is a livable, lovable home — a home in which 'to
> love, and to work, and to play, and to look up at the stars', a home
> for the children to enjoy and to thrive in, mentally and physically,
> and where my husband finds repose and courage.[24]

Hazel illustrated the article with her watercolor studies
of both the interior and exterior of their cottage. Another article in the same magazine followed in June, 1903, showing her
growing awareness of historical influences as reflected in the
various styles of southern California architecture. Hers was an
esoteric approach to analyzing the architecture where the
suitability of the site determined the individual design concept. She explained that many of the buildings portrayed a com-
monality in design origin. A similarity of design mirrored the
culture and custom of the times. According to Hazel, the
widespread influence of the past was apparent in the present
with an adaptation from that past to capture the flavor yet
modify with simplicity to modern needs. Hazel called attention to the utilization of color and appropriate types of land-
scaping as an aesthetic enhancement.[25]

Hazel Wood Waterman and daughter, 1902 (San Diego Historical Society).

Notes
Chapter Four

[1]Iris H.W. Engstrand, *San Diego: California's Cornerstone* (Tulsa: Continental Heritage Press, 1980), pp. 67-68.

[2]The Bancroft Library, Waterman Collection, letter from Waldo Waterman to Jane Waterman, San Diego, June 21, 1893.

[3]Waldo D. Waterman interview with Mary Jessop, January 25, 1970, p. 12. Typescript, SDHSRA

[4]Waldo D. Waterman interview with Mary Jessop, January 25, 1970, p. 13. Family Record, Waterman Line, 1758-1930. Typescript, SDHSRA.

[5]The Bancroft Library, Waterman Collection, letter from Hazel to Jane Waterman, June 28, 1894.

[6]The Bancroft Library, Waterman Collection. Contract to Waldo Waterman, 1894.

[7]The Bancroft Library, Waterman Collection, Waldo Waterman to Jane Waterman, San Diego, January 10, 1895.

[8]The Cabrillo celebration had begun in 1892 to honor Juan Rodriguez Cabrillo, discoverer of San Diego in 1542. See Sally Bullard Thornton, "San Diego's First Cabrillo Celebration," *Journal of San Diego History,* 30, (Summer 1984), pp. 167-180.

[9]The Bancroft Library, Waterman Collection, Hazel to Jane Waterman, San Diego, October 2, 1894.

[10]*Ibid.*

[11]The Bancroft Library, Waterman Collection, letter from Hazel to Waldo, San Francisco, March 10, 1896.

[12]Sylvia K. Flanigan, "Social and Intellectual Affiliation: Formation and Growth of San Diego's University Club," *The Journal of San Diego History,* 31, (Winter 1984), p. 42.

[13]*Ibid.,* p. 43.

[14]*Ibid.*

[15]*Ibid.,* pp. 45, 46.

[16]Waldo D. Waterman interview with Mary F. Ward, January 14, 1971, p. 3. Typescript, SDHSRA.

[17]Bruce Kamerling, "Irving Gill—The Artist as Architect," *The Journal of San Diego History,* 25, (Spring 1979), p. 159; Helen McElfresh Ferris, "Irving Gill, San Diego Architect 1870-1936, The Formation of An American Style of Architecture," *The Journal of San Diego History,* 41, (Fall 1971); Harriet Rochlin, "A Distinguished Generation of Women Architects in California," *A.I.A. Journal,* (August 1977), SDHSRA.

[18]Kamerling, "Irving Gill—The Artist as Architect," p. 158.

[19]*Ibid.*

[20]Waldo D. Waterman interview with Mary Jessop, January 25, 1970, p. 14. Typescript, SDHSRA; Waldo interview with Mary F. Ward, January 14, 1971, p. 3 Typescript, SDHSRA.

[21]Hazel Wood Waterman, "A Granite Cottage in California," *The House Beautiful,* 11, No. 4 (March 1902): pp. 245-250.

[22]Waldo D. Waterman interview with Mary Jessop, January 25, 1970, p. 15. Typescript SDHSRA; Waldo interview with Mary F. Ward, January 14, 1971, p. 3. Typescript, SDHSRA.

[23]Waterman, "A Granite Cottage in California," pp. 244-253.

[24]Waterman, "A Granite Cottage in California," p. 253.

[25]Hazel W. Waterman, "The Influence of an Olden Time," *The House Beautiful,* 14, No. 1 (June 1903): 3-9.

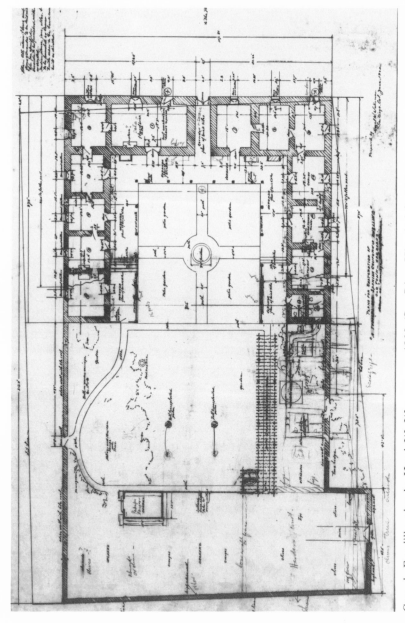

Casa de Estudillo, plan by Hazel W. Waterman, c. 1909 (San Diego Historical Society).

Chapter Five
Early Projects in San Diego

For ten years, Waldo managed to provide a good living for his family. In 1903, his untimely death at age forty-three shocked the community. Fortunately for the family, the railroad continued to be a source of revenue until 1916, when the Huntington, Spreckels people purchased it to further their San Diego Railway plans.[1]

Because many San Diego architects of the generation were produced by Hebbard and Gill, Hazel went to their office to discuss plans for her future. She met with Irving Gill to evaluate the possibility of entering into the study of architecture. Waldo had left her with a tidy life insurance policy and a share in San Diego, Cuyamaca and Eastern Railroad bonds. Nevertheless, Hazel had a mortgage on the house, and her three children were still in elementary school. She decided to fill the void in her life by developing an additional source of income which would eventually enable her to send the children to college. Gill suggested that she take an architectural course from the International Correspondence Schools since there were no architectural schools west of the Rockies.[2]

Hazel took Gill's advice and enrolled in basic courses in mechanical drawing and drafting. While she studied, she learned simple detail work by doing ink tracings on linen for Hebbard and Gill for a small salary. Hazel did all the work at home so she could maintain her household and raise her children. She quickly became proficient by spending up to five or six hours a day drafting.[3]

For approximately three years, Hazel associated with Hebbard and Gill, and worked hard at developing her designing skills. By 1906, at the age of forty-one, Hazel received her first commission from Alice Lee, a friend from the Wednesday Club. Miss Lee, a client of Irving Gill, recognized Hazel's talent and wanted her to do the architectural work on the construction of three new houses on Seventh. The construction site would be across the street from where the George Marston home at 3575 Seventh was being erected on the west rim of the canyon in Balboa Park. She felt that if it were not possible for her to be in charge, then Gill could supervise as the architect with Hazel doing the work. The arrangement proved to be successful. Miss Lee's delight with the completed structures immediately led to another request for Hazel's services.[4]

In 1908, Mr. William Clayton, Vice President and Managing Director of the Spreckels Companies, another satisfied client for whom Hazel had designed a beautiful home, selected her to restore the landmark Estudillo House known in those days as Ramona's Marriage Place.[5] Located in Old Town, the property had been purchased by Spreckels' San Diego Eastern Railroad Company. The house, originally constructed in 1829, was one of the oldest structures in present-day Old Town, San Diego. It had been occupied by the Estudillo family during the transitional period from Mexican to American rule. María Victoria Domínguez de Estudillo, widow of José María Estudillo and mother of eleven, lived in the home until her death in 1873.[6] After that time the home, from lack of care, began to suffer extensive damage.

The dilapidated remains of the Estudillo House served as a welcome challenge to Hazel for the restoration offered a complete departure from her previous projects. After visiting the long uninhabited site, she asked herself a number of questions:

What was here to make the preservation of this pathetic ruin worthwhile? Was there only an incident in a novel, a legend? Father Ubach[7] had told the author of "Ramona" [Helen Hunt Jackson] that once he had married an Indian to a fair skinned girl "in the chapel on the opposite side of the way." Father Ubach, who was like Father Gaspara in the novel . . . had lived in a house back of the Estudillo house that was more appealing to the imagination, and so in "Ramona" we read that "Father Gaspara's room was at the end of a long low adobe building, which . . . was now fallen into decay. . . .[8]

Hazel arduously pursued the task of researching how adobe structures were built during the Mexican period in California. She gleaned information that helped her develop ideas and plans from original manuscripts, old photographs, interviews with elderly Mexican and Spanish men and women. She decided the structure would be authentic in every detail from the foundation outward. She concerned herself with the precise method of preparing the materials and felt that the adobe brick should be made only by Mexican laborers who would prepare it by hand.[9] She personally visited

and examined all the remaining adobe buildings at Old Town, houses near Los Angeles, at Capistrano, and the Pico house at Whittier. The owners of Guajome, Santa Margarita, Penasquitos, and other ranches received me cordially, allowing me to take notes at their haciendas. I was enabled to examine the older work and to distinguish that of a later time. . . . In Los Angeles I had helpful conversation with Mr. Charles Lummis, and others whose interest in the early days was well known. . . . Plans, details, and specifications of a sort were prepared from those observations, notes, sketches, and studies.[10]

When restoration began, Hazel found that Abram Mendoza, a native workman, knew how to construct tiles and adobes "in the old way."[11] The preparation consisted of a composition of coarse gravel, stable straw, soft black clay and broken shells or seaweed kneaded carefully with bare hands. The workers shaped the mixture into bricks approximately sixteen inches long, eight inches wide and three inches thick. The moist bricks were baked for several weeks in the sun, being turned at least two times to prevent cracking. When dry and approved by the supervisor, they were put into place. Tile preparation required even more time since the clay had to be the consistency of soft putty before being rolled in trays and "dusted with sand" to prevent sticking. Once rolled to a thickness of nearly one inch, the portions were placed over wooden molds for shaping. From there they were placed in kilns and baked. Because the old walls had "cracked from top to bottom" and crumbled in different sections, they had to be bonded with sufficient adobe and broken tile to achieve the desired uniform thickness of four feet.[13]

Whenever possible, Hazel used left over material from the old building. Original and the undetectable new tiles were utilized to cover the room floors and the veranda roof. Specially antiqued veranda posts supported the ceiling constructed from "long slim canes of tule . . . woven with rawhide; above this is placed a thick layer of dry seaweed," on which the roof tiles rest.[14] Aside from being well seasoned, the red cedar, willow and redwood timbers used in construction also had special preparation requirements. They were "to be notched as if drawn by oxen — Red cedar to be round poles as nearly as possible of equal diameter throughout. Redwood to be hewn on three sides as if prepared in the forest, and by hand. This material to be prepared about eight weeks before placing, to be 'weathered' by exposure and dipping in mud and water and by any other process that may be expedient, and to be turned several times so that all sides will darken. . . .[15]

To substitute for the heavy roof timbers, "materials intended for wharf piles and telephone poles were provided by the Spreckels Company, cut to required dimensions, hand shaped and then aged by soaking in the mud flats of the bay."[16] The cactus juice recipe, used as an ingredient for the glue in the whitewash and mud plaster, called for "tuna or Castile Cactus (not wild cactus), the young leaves only," which were to be held on a spit over a flame (a row could be strung on a bar). Care had to be taken to keep them out of the ashes and dirt. The recipe continued:

> Scorch for about five minutes or until stickers are burned off and the skin blackened and the cactus becomes small and soft—Then mash them well, and put into a barrel until one half full and fill the barrel with water—Keep adding water or more cactus so that the substance forms a glue that will rope on a stick. Stir and let stand—It improves with standing some days and grows longer. It will peel off if too thick and should in that case be thinned with water. Run through a sieve when using it.[17]

There were no deviations from the original floor plan. Typically Hispanic, each room opened to the long low veranda that moved along the three-sided patio. The rooms were connected by doorways with the exception of the front entry which broke the inner connection in the center of the "U" shaped building. The irregular tile floors, the white walls, the peculiar Mexican blue stain of the woodwork were all similar to that which would have been found in the old house, as was the niche in the wall of the bedrooms for a crucifix or religious statue; and every bedroom had a single barred window facing the street side.[18]

The Estudillo project met with instant success and quickly became a showcase in San Diego. John Spreckels used the house to promote tours from his Hotel del Coronado. Guests and other tourists could ride on Spreckels' electric railway from downtown to the Old Town area. The house passed through several owners including Legler Benbough, who acquired the property and donated it to the State of California in 1968. It was further restored and furnished by the National Society of Colonial Dames of America in the State of California, San

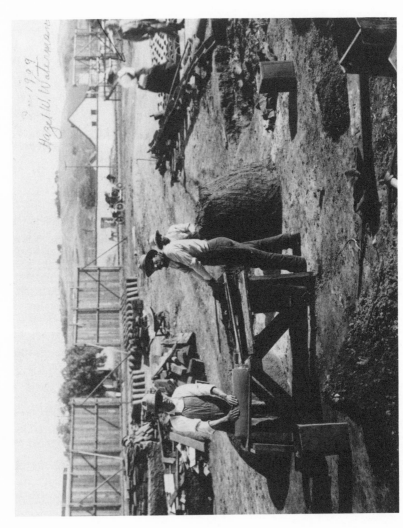

Casa de Estudillo, making roof tiles, c. 1909. Woman, in long dress at upper right, is believed to be Hazel Waterman (San Diego Historical Society).

Casa de Estudillo, making roof tiles, c. 1909 (San Diego Historical Society).

69

Casa de Estudillo, roof tiles, c. 1909 (San Diego Historical Society).

Casa de Estudillo, reconstruction, c. 1909 (San Diego Historical Society).

Casa de Estudillo, bricks drying, c. 1909 (San Diego Historical Society).

Casa de Estudillo, reconstructing the roof, c. 1909 (San Diego Historical Society).

Casa de Estudillo, side view, c. 1909 (San Diego Historical Society).

Casa de Estudillo, rear view, c. 1909 (San Diego Historical Society).

Ground plan, Casa de Estudillo (San Diego Historical Society).

Casa de Estudillo, gardens, c. 1918 (San Diego Historical Society).

Diego County Committee under the direction of Mary Belcher Farrell, Chairman of the furnishing committee. She worked with Frances V. Wagaman Tallman to acquire authentic period pieces.[19]

The Estudillo restoration led to another notable accomplishment in design. Hazel, a member of the Wednesday Club since the late 1880s, had earned the confidence of the membership in many ways. She had served on the Board for four years, been a Vice President and had already given eight of the twelve papers she presented before the group. Hazel's intellectual interests were vast, and she selected a wide range of subjects to explore and take before her club sisters. Her papers were interesting and those that were co-authored with friends were quite esoteric in nature. Through her years of association with the Wednesday Club, Hazel offered the following variety of well-developed research:

> 1898 Topic for the year *California,* paper: "Romance and Tragedy in Transition Days."
>
> 1900 paper on "Christian Socialism"
>
> 1901 paper on "Problems Evolved from the Study of Faust."
>
> 1902 paper on "Arts and Crafts of Early England" with Alice Klauber
>
> 1903 paper on "Ophelia, Isabella and Portia," with Charlotte Woodward
>
> 1903 paper on the "Present Problems in the Social Economy"
>
> 1905 paper on "Prints and Stencils of Japan" with Alice Klauber
>
> 1910 Topic for year: *Evolution of Greek Drama,* paper: "Attic Theatre and the Function of the Chorus," with Bessie Peery

Alice Klauber (San Diego Historical Society).

1911   Topic for year: *Evolution of Literature: Rome,* paper:
       "The Rostrum"
1915   paper on "Festival Spirit and the Exposition"
1915   Topic for year *California,* paper: "The Universities,"
       with Adele Meyer Outcalt
1915   paper on "Rabindranath Tagor," with Mrs. White
       and Mrs. Wangenheim.[20]

Hazel had another term as vice president in 1915-1916.
During that same year, she served on the program committee.[21]

With the urging of Alice Lee, the Wednesday Club asked
Hazel to design and construct their new building to be erected
at Sixth and Ivy Lane.[22] The club members felt the building
should ". . . be useful and suitable for . . . meetings . . . "
and ". . . provide a dignified assembly room for social gather-
ings for . . . members . . . families and friends, and for con-
certs, lectures, and parties by the general public."[23] Hazel asked
her friend, club member and interior design student Alice
Klauber to assist her with the decor. The plans were studied
by an appointed plans committee comprised of Miss Lee, Mrs.
George Marston and Mrs. Ernest White. Mrs. Marston
reported that Mrs. White helped with details which enhanced
the attractiveness and suitability of the structure. The prelim-
inary plans which Hazel submitted to the club in May, 1910,
met with such enthusiasm that she "was authorized to complete them." The final plans were submitted and adopted in
July. The plans committee then became the "building committee, with the admonition to make any changes which would
reduce the cost without sacrificing beauty and convenience;
but so carefully had the plans been drawn that the committee
decided against any change whatsoever."[24]

To pay for the building, the committee was charged with
the responsibility of developing a fund-raising plan. They were
able to mortgage the lot for $7,500, secure $4,500 from club

The Wednesday Club, Sixth and Ivy, San Diego, c. 1930 (San Diego Historical Society).

members who subscribed to interest-bearing bonds, and sell
the old club house for $3,100. The purchaser paid $1,100 in
cash and assumed the mortgage for the balance. Hazel "donated
$50 of her fee for the caravel tiles which she and Miss Klauber
selected for the front of the building, while the open work tiles
within were designed by Hazel."[25]

Hazel complied with the club's wishes by designing the
one-story flat roof building with a half-story over the assembly
hall.[26] She used California talents such as sculptor, Anna Valen-
tien, who created the etched door hardware and brass-framed
art glass lantern on the outside, and ceramist, Ernest Batch-
elder, who developed the tile work.[27] The entire job was completed quickly so that by April 26, 1911, the Wednesday Club
members could open their new building for a celebration.[28]

Notes
Chapter Five

[1]Return of a Death (certificate), Waldo Sprague Waterman, San Diego, California, July 24, 1903. County Recorders Office, County Administration Building. Family Record, Waterman Line, 1758-1930. Typescript, SDHSRA. Waldo D. Waterman interview with Mary Jessop, January 25, 1970, pp. 12, 13. Typescript, SDHSRA.

[2]Waldo D. Waterman interview with Mary Jessop, January 25, 1970, pp. 14, 15. Typescript, SDHSRA. Waldo D. Waterman interview with Mary F. Ward, January 14, 1971, p. 4. Typescript, SDHSRA; Waldo D. Waterman interview with Mary F. Ward, January 14, 1971, p. 4. Typescript, SDHSRA. Harriet Rochlin, "Among the First and the Finest: California Architects: Julia, Hazel, Lillian, Lutah, Elda," pp. 6, 7. Typescript, SDHSRA; Harriet Rochlin, "A Distinguished Generation of Women Architects in California," *AIA Journal,* (August 1977).

[3]Waldo D. Waterman interview with Mary Jessop, January 25, 1970, p. 15. Typescript, SDHSRA; Waldo D. Waterman interview with Mary F. Ward, January 14, 1971, p. 4. Typescript, SDHSRA.

[4]Hazel in fact commanded the entire project. Waldo D. Waterman interview with Mary Jessop, January 25, 1970, p. 15. Typescript, SDHSRA. Waldo D. Waterman interview with Mary F. Ward, January 14, 1971, p. 6. Typescript, SDHSRA.

[5]The name Ramona's Marriage Place evolved from the novel *Ramona* written by Helen Hunt Jackson in 1884. Jackson's book created a tremendous interest in the mistreatment of the Indians. Jackson led an effective campaign to press for reform. Andrew F. Rolle, *California, A History* (Arlington Heights, Illinois: A.H.M. Publishing Corporation, 1978), p. 365; W. Clayton to Mrs. H.W. Waterman, March 7, 1910. Typescript, SDHSRA.

[6]Engstrand, *San Diego: California's Cornerstone,* p. 39.

[7]Father Antonio Ubach served as a priest in San Diego during the 1880s and had sponsored a school for Indians. See Engstrand, *San Diego: California's Cornerstone,* pp. 54-55.

[8]Hazel Wood Waterman, "The Restoration of a Landmark," pp. 1, 2. Typescript, SDHSRA.

[9]Hazel W. Waterman, "Part of Specifications used on restoration of old adobe building at Old Town." Typescript, SDHSRA. "Views Alone Worth Visit," *Los Angeles Times,* March, 1910; "Landmarks Draw Much Attention," *Los Angeles Times,* March 8, 1910; D.E. Kessler, "The Restoration of Ramona's Marriage Place," *The Pacific Monthly,* Portland, Oregon, (June 1910), pp. 585-588; "La Suen," "Ramona's Marriage Place," *West Coast Magazine,* Los Angeles, (August 1910); Isabel Frazee, "The Restoration at Old San Diego of the Estudillo House, popularly known as the marriage place of Ramona," *The Federation Courier,* Berkeley, California, February 1911; Hazel W. Waterman, "The Restoration of a Landmark," Typescript, SDHSRA.

[10]Lummis, writer and librarian at the Los Angeles Public Library, was a promoter of California's Hispanic heritage. He had built an adobe home called El Alisal, presently headquarters of the Historical Society of Southern California; Waterman, "The Restoration of a Landmark," p. 4.

[11]Winifred Davidson Notes, 1934, and Frazee, "The Restoration at Old San Diego of the Estudillo House," p. 2, SDHSRA.

[12]*Ibid.*

[13]*Ibid.*

[14]Frazee, "The Restoration at Old San Diego of the Estudillo House," p. 2.

[15]*Ibid.*

[16]Waterman, *Restoration of a Landmark,* p. 6.

[17]Frazee, "The Restoration at Old San Diego of the Estudillo House," p. 30.

[18]*Ibid.*

[19]All American items were of the pre-1850 period and had come around Cape Horn during the Mexican Period. The house, an ongoing project, is today open to the public in Old Town State Park.

[20]Sarah W. Spiess, "Wednesday Club Papers given by Hazel W. Waterman from 1898-1920, and offices held as compiled from yearbooks." Typescript, The Wednesday Club Archives, San Diego, California.

[21]The Wednesday Club, "An Historical Sketch, 1895-1928," SDHSRA.

[22]*Ibid.*

[23]*Ibid.*

[24]*Ibid.*

[25]*Ibid.*

[26]*Ibid.*

[27]Robert Miles Parker, "Reflections, The Wednesday Club," *Downtown San Diego,* September 14, 1981.

[28]The Wednesday Club, "An Historical Sketch, 1895-1928," SDHSRA.

Project for a residence, design and sketch by Hazel W. Waterman (San Diego Historical Society).

Chapter Six
Later Architectural Accomplishments

B<small>Y THE TIME</small> the Wednesday Club was finished in the spring of 1911, Hazel had already begun plans for a sizable residence in the exclusive Bankers' Hill area at 3170 Curlew Street. The four-story house was designed for Captain and Mrs. Albert A. Ackerman, United States Navy retired, who would live there until about 1922.[1] It was uniquely situated on the south side of the street and took advantage of the beautiful San Diego harbor view. The interior design featured many new household conveniences such as a clothes chute from the top floor to the laundry room two floors below; a dumbwaiter from the kitchen to the laundry room; a central vacuum system; an indoor drying area in the furnace room; and a built-in refrigerator alcove.[2]

Hazel, always concerned about human comfort, designed staircase landings to ease the strain of the climb. At the top floor landing, on the north side, there was an attractive arched, colored glass window which allowed for light and privacy. The kitchen was conveniently located at the northeast corner, adjacent to the butler's pantry. For entertainment purposes, a ballroom was located on the first story below the main floor.

The bottom basement had a dirt floor and was used for storage of trunks, gardening tools and other equipment. To facilitate automobile maintenance, a rectangular cement pit was recessed in the floor of the single car garage located to the west of the laundry room in a separate building. Beneath the garage was a small storage room where the exterior of the recessed pit could be seen.[3]

The home still has the largest garden in the area. Hazel

Residence for Captain and Mrs. Albert A. Ackerman, front view, c. 1912 (San Diego Historical Society).

Ackerman residence, rear view, c. 1912 (San Diego Historical Society).

terraced the side of the hill with stones from the San Diego
beaches. The terraces, located on the sunny south side of the
property had beds for flowers, shrubs, citrus and fruit trees.
Angular dirt pathways and cement stairs faced with rock led
to and from the garden at the bottom of the large lot. The
pathways extended through the garden to the rim of a small,
very deep canyon in the property. On the east side, Hazel
designed an attractive pergola for climbing roses.[4] She engaged
the architectural firm of Bristow and Lyman to complete the
supervision of the building during the final period so that she
could go to the University of California at Berkeley to attend
architectural lecture courses.[5]

While constructing the Ackerman house, Hazel had
already drawn plans and begun the work on the building for
babies for the Children's Home Association of San Diego in
Balboa Park. Later in 1926, the organization engaged her to
design and erect their three-story administration building which
also housed sleeping areas, a dining room, kitchen, auditorium
and reception rooms. Comments regarding her architectural
achievement are best portrayed by the following candid state-
ments that reflected the general reaction to the building:

> . . . this could be a lovely villa on the Mediterranean . . . it seems
> like a dream home, and yet it is a real one. It has all a mother's heart
> would dream and plan for her own children. Only a loving mother-
> thought could make it possible.[6]

Several years before Hazel received the final Children's
Home commission, she designed a magnificent garden for
Julius and Laura (Klauber) Wangenheim. The Wangenheims,
long active in business and social circles in San Diego, wanted
a unique garden showplace.[7] Hazel incorporated ideas from
English and Italian gardens stressing beauty, warmth and
privacy. She created a fountain, pools, terraces, brick walls,
and complemented them with flowers and luxurious foliage.[8]

Garden for Julius Wangenheim, designed by Hazel W. Waterman (San Diego Historical Society).

Cottage for Babies, Hazel W. Waterman architect (San Diego Historical Society).

Childrens Home Association, Administration Building. Hazel W. Waterman architect (San Diego Historical Society).

93

For this achievement, Hazel received a Certificate of Honor from the San Diego Chapter of the American Institute of Architects.[9]

Continued success increased the demand on Hazel's time. Although she had completed correspondence courses, Hazel failed to become a licensed architect. Friends encouraged her to apply to the California State Board of Architecture for a license. Several prominent people sent letters of endorsement to the Board on her behalf.[10] Letters from the Board to Hazel in 1914, indicate they had received samples of her work, and would waive the written examinations if she would just appear in person. Hazel did not take time to go to Los Angeles to complete the requirements. Twenty years later, in 1934, Hazel penciled on the Board's last letter, a notation which said, "I regret very much that I did not respond. I never applied again."[11]

Hazel gave four more papers before the Wednesday Club prior to becoming president in 1920-21 during their Silver Anniversary Year.[12] Although she continued design work, Hazel concentrated her professional efforts on homes for her children, Helen and Waldo, and brother, Judge Walton J. Wood.[13] In her later years, Hazel retired to live in Berkeley at the Berkeley City Women's Club[14] where she became a member of their Writers' Section. She spent her time writing and traveling to Europe and the West Indies until she passed away on January 22, 1948, at eighty-two years of age.[15]

Hazel Waterman's contributions to California architecture and design have never gone out of date. Her architectural philosophy is best summarized in an article which she wrote for *The Federation* in January, 1921, entitled "The Figure of the House."[16] In it she discussed what she considered to be the thoughtful, intelligent approach to home design. For Hazel, the basic ingredients for the development of successful living conditions are brought together with the cooperation of the architect, home owner, builder, and interior decorator. Only then could the finished product meet all her criteria, with a thoroughly modern attitude.

Hazel noted that the site selected should provide family members with accessibility to their individual endeavors. Special considerations were to be given to the location of the view, the position of the sun, and the condition of the soil. From these essentials, the floor plan of the house could be worked to maximize the best from these elements. The appropriate form and architectural style chosen were important to the esthetic concept at each step. This provided the backdrop for the total setting. The garden layout or juxtaposition of the paths, drives, walkways and the plantings, which included trees and hedges were necessary to complete the exterior plan.

All artistic endeavors had to fit to scale, as did the development of the interior plan for color, furniture design and placement, and window treatments. Hazel expressed concern for the complexities involved with the degree of sophistication of the owners' refined or common taste. This might also involve their habits or simple sentimental attachments which would be reflected in the home. The architect pressed to sympathetically orient and develop the client's awareness of how each design component would become an integral part of the others to achieve internal and external balance.

All too often, according to Hazel, the well-meaning interior decorator might "be considered extraordinarily artistic, and yet lack architectural unity or the essential homelike quality . . . The house furnished entirely by the architect or by an interior decorator falls short of being the ideal home." For her, there was an art to designing a home that was comfortable, functional, attractive, and reflected the homeowners' personality.[17]

Throughout her life, Hazel remained active with the same drive and pioneer spirit which gave her distinction as the second female architect in California.[18] Hazel Wood Waterman, a truly talented and caring person, had dedicated herself to a philosophy of concern for the comfort and well being of others. In all her activities, as well as in her family life, she also exemplified the determination required to achieve greatness in the second half of life's cycle. She would have been a remarkable woman in any age.

Hazel W. Waterman's "cottage design from a barn" for Mrs. Geo. Barney, c. 1909 (San Diego Historical Society).

97

Residence for William Clayton (garden side) San Diego, Sixth and Laurel, by Hazel W. Waterman (San Diego Historical Society).

A "Rendering for the Wednesday Club House, 1911" by Hazel W. Waterman (San Diego Historical Society).

A house in Mexico? by Hazel W. Waterman (San Diego Historical Society).

Hazel W. Waterman's sketch for Children's Home, San Diego (San Diego Historical Society).

101

Notes
Chapter Six

[1]The Third Annual Historical Homes Tour — Bankers' Hill (a portion thereof), SDHSRA pamphlet, 1972.

[2]Personal observation of the author as a resident in the home, 1944-1950.

[3]*Ibid.*

[4]*Ibid.*

[5]Letter from A.A. Ackerman to H.W. Waterman, San Diego, California, December 10, 1912, SDHSRA.

[6]Matilda Hunt, "A Home for Children," p. 6. Typescript, SDHSRA. Hazel W. Waterman to Miss Bernice Cosgrove, President and Board of Directors of the San Diego Children's Home Association, Berkeley, California, October 2, 1946, SDHSRA.

[7]The Wangenheims had arrived in San Diego in 1896 from San Francisco. Julius Wangenheim was in the wholesale grocery business and later purchased a controlling interest in the Bank of Commerce of San Diego. He was long active in civic development. See Carl H. Heilbron, *History of San Diego County* (San Diego: San Diego Press Club, 1936), pp. 156-157.

[8]Hazel W. Waterman, "A City Garden in Southern California, Possessing the Charm of Adaptability to the Out-of-Door Habits of Life," *House and Garden,* August, 1920.

[9]The San Diego Chapter of the American Institute of Architects, Certificate of Honor to Mrs. Hazel Waterman (architect), ". . . to recognize merit in design and execution of work in Architecture and Fine Arts. . .judged by a competent jury." Garden of Mr. and Mrs. Julius Wangenheim, June 29, 1933. SDHSRA.

[10]W. Clayton to California State Board of Architecture, San Diego, California, November 12, 1913; Mrs. George Marston to California State Board of Architecture, San Diego, California, December 12, 1913; Caroline W. Darling to California State Board of Architecture, San Diego, California, December 27, 1913; Mrs. Evelyn Lawson to California State Board of Architecture, San Diego, California, December 27, 1913. SDHSRA.

[11]Fred'k L. Roehrig to Mrs. Waterman, Los Angeles, California, January 30, 1914; Fred'k L. Roehrig to Mrs. Waterman, Los Angeles, California, October 20, 1914. Note: This document includes penciled notation dated 1934 and initialed H.W.W. SDHSRA.

[12]Sarah W. Spiess, "Wednesday Club Papers given by Hazel W. Waterman from 1898-1920, and offices held, as compiled from yearbook." Typescript, The Wednesday Club Archives, San Diego, California.

[13]Waterman Notebook, "Buildings designed and developed by Hazel Wood Waterman." Typescript, SDHSRA. Judge Walton J. Wood to Mrs. Hazel W. Waterman, Los Angeles, California, June 7, 1929. SDHSRA.

[14]The Berkeley City Women's Club, designed by Hazel's contemporary, Julia Morgan, California's first woman architect, offered a logical location for Hazel's continuous intellectual pursuits.

[15]Obituaries, *Berkeley Daily Gazette,* January 23, 1948, p. 14.

[16]The magazine was one "published in the Interest of Organizations Devoted to the Betterment of Social and Civic Life."

[17]Hazel Wood Waterman, "The Figure of the House," *The Federation,* (January 1910).

[18]Harriet Rochlin, "A Distinguished Generation of Women Architects in California," *AIA Journal* (August, 1977). SDHSRA.

Appendix

Buildings designed and developed
by Hazel Wood Waterman

for

1. Miss Alice Pratt — cottage?	1906
2. Mrs. Geo. Barney — cottage developed from a barn	1907
3. Resience for Mr. and Mrs. Wm. Clayton — (from a water color sketch by ? Architect alteration for a third floor	1909
4. Residence for Mrs. Smith and Miss Friese	1908-1909
6. The Wednesday Club House Sept 1910 to June 1911	
5. Restoration of Estudillo House Miscalled Ramona's Marriage Place	1909
7. Garden for Julius Wangenheim — 1911 or 1917? ?Garden Wall for Titus — Coronado	
8. Residences for Capt and Mrs. A.A. Ackerman	1912?
10. Residences (cottage) for Mrs. Churcher at La Jolla	1914-1915?
9. Home for Babies (at Childrens Home)	1912?
10. Shop building for Lucy Newkirk	1923?
11. Leisenring Res.	1920
Children's Home (Administration Building)	1924
Assisted Helen W. Kincaide Palos Verdes	192
Residence Judge Walton J. Wood	1928-9
Cottage for Waldo Dean Waterman	1929?
Alterations — Steven's Residence, Coronado	
Mrs. Iva N. Lawson — Library	
Capt. Hines — Coronado	
Miss Alice Holliday	
Dr. and Mrs. H.G. Leisenring	

Made drawings for residences
Mr. and Mrs. Vernon Matthews
Mr. and Mrs. Charles Powell
    but these were not built because of
    changes in the lives and finances of the
    clients.
Assisted Irving J. Gill with the
    following residences —
    Miss Alice Lee
    Miss Teats
    Miss and Mrs. Geo. Hawley
    Dr. Goff —
Also made sketch plans for
    Miss Elizabeth Frazee
Sketch studies for stations (Mission Cliff
Gardens and Rey — Electric)
Sketch studies for Mrs. Stephens

Note: This appendix is reproduced exactly as it was hand-written by Hazel Wood Waterman in the original document.

Waterman File, SDHSRA — Hazel was 41 in 1906 when she began her second career and 64 in 1929, when she completed the cottage for her son Waldo Dean Waterman.

Bibliography

Manuscripts:

Legler Benbough, Private Collection

Miscellaneous Letters, Notes and Documents, The Waterman Collection. The Bancroft Library, Berkeley, California.

Miscellaneous Notes and Documents, The Waterman File, San Diego Historical Society Research Archives, San Diego, California. Hereinafter SDHSRA.

Letters:

A.A. Ackerman to H.W. Waterman, San Diego, California, December 10, 1912. SDHSRA.

W. Clayton to California State Board of Architecture, San Diego, California, November 12, 1913. SDHSRA.

W. Clayton to Mrs. H.H. Waterman, March 7, 1910. SDHSRA.

Caroline W. Darling to California State Board of Architecture, San Diego, California, December 27, 1913. SDHSRA.

Salvador R. Estudillo to Mrs. Hazel W. Waterman, San Diego, California, July 30, 1909. SDHSRA.

Mrs. Evelyn Lawson to California State Board of Architecture, San Diego, California, December 27, 1913. SDHSRA.

Charles F. Lummis to Mrs. Hazel W. Waterman, May 25, 1908. SDHSRA.

Mrs. George Marston to California State Board of Architecture, San Diego, California, December 12, 1913. SDHSRA.

Fred'k L. Roehrig to Mrs. Waterman, Los Angeles, California, January 30, 1914; Fred'k L. Roehrig to Mrs. Waterman, Los Angeles, California, October 20, 1914. SDHSRA.

Julius Wangenheim to Mrs. Waldo S. Waterman, San Diego, California, March 17, 1917. SDHSRA.

Hazel H. Waterman to Miss Bernice Cosgrove, President and Board of Directors of the San Diego Childrens' Home Association, Berkeley, California, October 2, 1946. SDHSRA.

Judge Walton J. Wood to Mrs. Hazel W. Waterman, Los Angeles, California, June 7, 1929. SDHSRA.

Typescripts:

San Diego Historical Society Research Archives. Hereinafter SDHSRA.

Davidson, Winifred. Notes, 1934, on Isabel Frazee's article on Estudillo House Restoration.

Family Record, Waterman Line, 1758-1930. Typescript, SDHSRA.

Hunt, Matilda, "A Home for Children." Typescript, SDHSRA.

Jasper, James A. "Trail-Breakers and History-Makers of Julian, Ballena, Mesa Grande, Oak Grove, Warner Ranch, Banner, Cuyamaca, in San Diego County, California," Vol. 2. Typescript, SDHSRA.

Lamb, Charles A. "Restoration of Casa de Estudillo," January 1971. Typescript, SDHSRA.

Rochlin, Harriet. "Among the First and the Finest: California Architects: Julia, Hazel, Lillian, Lutah, Elda." Typescript, SDHSRA.

Spiess, Sarah W. "Hazel Waterman, Architect of the Wednesday Club," February 1979. Typescript, Wednesday Club Archives.

Spiess, Sarah H. "Wednesday Club Papers given by Hazel W. Waterman from 1898-1920, and offices held as compiled from yearbooks." Typescript, The Wednesday Club Archives, San Diego, California.

Taylor, Dan Forrest. "Julian Gold," F.E.C. Federal Writers' Project, San Diego, California, February 8, 1939. Typescript, SDHSRA.

Ward, Mary F. "Hazel Wood Waterman Biographical Information," from interviews with Waldo Dean Waterman, San Diego, California, May 5, 1971. Typescript, SDHSRA.

Waterman, Hazel H. "Part of Specifications used on restoration of old adobe building at Old Town." Typescript, SDHSRA.

Waterman, Hazel H. 'The Restoration of a Landmark.' Typescript, SDHSRA.

Waterman Notebook. "Buildings designed and developed by Hazel Wood Waterman."

The Wednesday Club. "An Historical Sketch, 1895-1928."

Newspapers:

Obituaries, *Berkeley Daily Gazette,* January 23, 1984, p. 14.

The Chico Record, July 7, 1935; July 12, 1936; May 17, 1936 (Meriam Library, California State University, Chico, California).

Obituary, W.R. Waterman, *San Francisco Examiner,* April 13, 1891.

Los Angeles Times, March 1910.

Los Angeles Times, March 8, 1910.

The San Diego Union, October 20, 1907.

Interviews:

Sam Hamill interview with Bob Wright assisted by Waunita Wills, San Diego, California, August 24, 1974. SDHSRA.

Waldo D. Waterman interview with Mary Jessop, January 25, 1970.

Waldo D. Waterman interview with Mary F. Ward, January 14, 1971.

Public Archives:

Certified Copy of Death Record, Robert Whitney Waterman, San Diego, April 12, 1891. County Recorders Office, County Administration Building.

Probate Files for Robert W. Waterman, no. 775, Waldo S. Waterman, no. 2502, Robert Wood Waterman, no. 2501, San Diego, California, Superior Court Archives.

Return of a Death, Waldo Sprague Waterman, San Diego, California, July 24, 1903. County Recorders Office, City Administration Building.

Books:

Ellsberg, Helen. *Mines of Julian.* Glendale, California: La Siesta Press, 1972.

Engstrand, Iris H.W. *San Diego: California's Cornerstone.* Tulsa: Continental Heritage Press, 1980.

Heilbron, Carl H. *History of San Diego County.* San Diego: San Diego Press Club, 1936.

Johl, Karen. *Timeless Treasures: San Diego's Victorian Heritage.* San Diego: Rand Editions, 1982.

History of Julian. Julian: Julian Historical Society, 1969.

Kostof, Spiro, Ed. *The Architect.* New York: Oxford University Press, 1977.

Melendy H. Bret, and Benjamin F. Gilbert. *Governors of California.* Georgetown, California: The Talisman Press, 1965.

Moyer, Cecil. *Historic Ranchos of San Diego.* Edited by Richard Pourade. San Diego: Union-Tribune Publishing Company [A Copley Book], 1969.

Pourade, Richard. *The History of San Diego: The Glory Years.* San Diego: Union Tribune Publishing Company [A Copley Book], 1964.

Rolle, Andrew F. *California: A History.* Arlington Heights, Illinois: A.H.M. Publishing Co., 1978.

Wells, Harry L., and W.L. Chambers. *History of Butte County, California.* Two volumes in One. San Francisco: Harry L. Wells, 1882, pp. 304, 305.

Yearbook. University of California. 1886.

Articles:

Berkeley City Women's Club, "Club Journalette."

Berkeley City Women's Club, "50th Anniversary 1927-1977," Berkeley, California.

Ferris, Helen McElfresh. "Irving John Gill, San Diego Archi-

tect 1870-1936, The Formation of an American Style of Architecture," *The Journal of San Diego History,* Vol. XVII, No. 41,
Fall 1971.

Flanigan, Sylvia K. "Social and Intellectual Affiliation: Formation and Growth of San Diego's University Club," *The
Journal of San Diego History,* Vol. XXXI, No. 1, Winter 1984,
pp. 40-50.

Frazee, Isabel. "The Restoration of Old San Diego of the
Estudillo House, popularly known as the marriage place of
Ramona," *The Federation Courier,* Berkeley, California,
February 1911.

Kamerling, Bruce. "Irving Gill—The Artist as Architect," *The
Journal of San Diego History,* Vol. XXV, No. 2, Spring 1979,
pp. 151-188.

Kessler, D.E. "The Restoration of Ramona's Marriage Place,"
The Pacific Monthly, Portland, Oregon, June 1910, pp.
585-588.

"La Suen," "Ramona's Marriage Place," *West Coast Magazine,* Los
Angeles, August 1910.

Parker, Robert Miles. "Reflections, The Wednesday Club,"
Downtown San Diego, September 14, 1981.

"Our Contributors," *The Federation,* January 1921.

Rochlin, Harriet. "A Distinguished Generation of Women
Architects in California," *A.I.A. Journal,* August 1977,
SDHSRA.

Thornton, Sally Bullard. "San Diego's First Cabrillo Celebration," *The Journal of San Diego History,* Summer, 1984, pp.
167-180.

Waterman, Hazel W. "A City Garden in Southern California, Possessing the Charm of Adaptability to the Out-of-Door Habits of Life," *House and Garden,* August 1920.

Waterman, Hazel W. "A Granite Cottage in California," *The House Beautiful,* Vol. 11, No. 4, March, 1902, pp. 244-253.

Waterman, Hazel W. "The Influence of an Olden Time," *The House Beautiful,* Vol. 14, No. 1, June, 1903, pp. 3-9.

Miscellaneous:

The Third Annual Historical Homes Tours — Banker's Hill (a portion thereof). Pamphlet, 1972.

Index

A Note About the Author

SALLY BULLARD THORNTON, a
native San Diegan and one-time cham-
pion equestrian, graduated from high
school at the age of sixteen in Columbia, Missouri, where she received an
A.A. degree from Stephens College. She
graduated from the University of San
Diego with a B.A. and an M.A. in history. The recipient of three Institute of
History awards, she has published in
The Journal of San Diego History and con-
tributed to several other publications.
Long active as a community volunteer,
she has held numerous leadership posi-
tions, and received many awards for her
accomplishments. She is on the Board
of Directors of Micom Systems, Inc. and
Medical Materials, Inc. She is listed in
Who's Who in California and is president
of The John M. and Sally B. Thornton
Foundation and vice president of the
San Diego Museum of Art.